AFFIRMATIONS AND ANTIDOTES

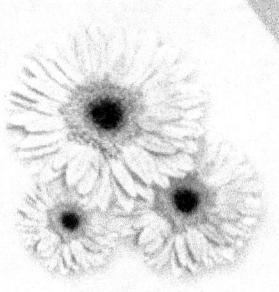

AFFIRMATIONS and ANTIDOTES

That Strengthen ME

words of wisdom, guidance and inspiration

AFFIRMATIONS AND ANTIDOTES
THE STRENGHTEN ME

words of wisdom, guidance and inspiration

© 2018 Marilyn E. Porter

All Rights Reserved.
This book or any portion thereof may not be reproduced or used in any manner whatsoever without the express written permission of the publisher except for the use of brief quotations in a book review.

ISBN 13: 978-0-9991837-7-9
ISBN-10: 0-9991837-7-X

SBG MEDIA GROUP
ATLANTA

Printed in the United States of America

Marilyn Elizabeth Porter "M.E." is a woman confidently and intentionally living her purpose: bringing light and wisdom to the world. She makes no apologies for being a woman of unflappable faith and allows her Christianity to shine brightly in every arena. Although there are many titles and descriptions that fit her, "Mommy" is one of her most prized accolades. Her God and her children (in that order) have been the driving forces in her life.

Dr. Porter is the Apostolic Visionary, Founder, and Leader of The Pink Pulpit Crusade International—a ministry birthed to cover, train, and encourage other women in ministry. The Pink Pulpit is a ministry resource for the "Called" and the "Chosen". The motto is: "Let's Pain the Whole World PINK!"—being a picture of God's love.

She is most widely known for her work as a Spiritual Life Coach, Author, and in Ministry Development. "M.E." now stands alone in a very sacred and savvy space as "The Scatter-Brained Genius' Coach". Her journey to this place—that is, The Scatter-Brained Genius' Coach—has been a colorful one that has quite a few pitstops and pitfalls. KNOWING her gifts was the easy part; knowing how to use them, grow them, and monetize them has not been so easy. However, over the course of seven years, she has been able to successfully translate her GENIUS into $$$s and takes great pleasure in helping others do the same!

AFFIRMATIONS AND ANTIDOTES

"I AM UNFLAPPABLE!"

"For he will be like a tree planted by the water, that extends its roots by a stream. And will not fear when the heat comes; but its leaves will be green, and it will not be anxious in a year of drought nor cease to yield fruit."

Jeremiah 17:8 (NASB)

"And he will be like a tree firmly planted [and fed] by streams of water, which yields its fruit in its season; its leaf does not wither; and in whatever he does, he prospers [and comes to maturity]."

Psalm 1:3 (AMP)

The Antidote

In reading the scripture passages provided, you will see my concept of what it means to be UNFLAPPABLE.

I recall as a child, there was a toy called 'Weebles' and the slogan was "Weebles wobble, but they don't fall down!" I may be dating myself a little, but I remember those commercials as though I'd just seen it yesterday. I also remember thinking that I could relate to the mighty 'Weeble' because even at a very young age, I had already endured some things that would have knocked down the average adult. Yet, I was still standing—unmoved, unscrambled, and yes...I was and am UNFLAPPABLE.

For many years of my life, I was the judge of 'flappableness' (not sure if it is a word, but since these are my thoughts, I am going to make it a word). I would listen to people whine and complain about things that, in all truth, we MAJOR. As for me, I viewed the expressions of pain and struggle as a sign of ultimate weakness. Dare I say that I was surrounded by weaklings? After all, everyone has tough times and life issues to deal with...except for me (or so I thought).

Without going into great detail, I will get right to the point of this antidote: There is a very distinct difference between being UNFLAPPABLE and being NUMB! Unfortunately, they look the same on the outside. It is the heart of the matter that determines the difference.

I must confess to you that the early years—perhaps the first 20 years of my adulthood—were not UNFLAPPABLE years; they were numb years. I was not merely unmoved by things, people, and situations; I was incapable of feeling anything that would cause me to flap. I was disconnected from anything emotional (or shall I say anything that could possibly cause me pain). Please know

AFFIRMATIONS AND ANTIDOTES

that numbness and the inability to cope with or process negative emotions does not make you planted, rooted, or unflappable: It makes you a shell of a human being.

It was the amazing grace of the Savior that awakened me to the truth that I was broken in so many places in my heart that I was unable to feel. I was numb, and that state was, in all actuality, putting me in greater danger than feeling the pain. See, when you are numb, you will sit in the midst of pain and not even know that it is hurting you! If you have ever had a tooth pulled or any dental work whereby the dentist gave you a Novocain shot to numb your mouth, then you know that during that time of numbness, they tell you not to eat because you could actually chew your jaw or bite your tongue—and not even know it until you are able to feel again!

I have sat in so much pain, unaware of its effects on my mind, body, and soul...all the while believing I was just strong and immovable. NOT! My dear one, let me assure you that only the love and healing virtue of Jesus can position you and I to be truly UNFLAPPABLE.

UNFLAPPABLE does not mean I don't get my feelings hurt. UNFLAPPABLE does not mean I don't get lied on or cheated on. UNFLAPPABLE does not mean I always get it right. UNFLAPPABLE does not mean I don't cry or even find myself a little depressed at times. UNFLAPPABLE does not mean I am always loved, always respected, always honored, and always acknowledged.

UNFLAPPABLE means that I am solid in the BEING of whom GOD has called me to BE and that I can do all that He has called me to do—regardless of the feelings I have to push through to walk in His will for my life.

NEVERTHELESS, I AM UNFLAPPABLE!

Sharetta Small Donalson is a native of Canton, Mississippi. She is currently serving in the healthcare field as a Registered Nurse. She is an admired Mentor and Certified Christian Life Coach to women from various walks of life. She encourages and gives wisdom through her life's challenges and the Word of God. Some of that wisdom was shared on a broader spectrum in her debut book, Forgiveness: The Quest for Healing Your Heart. In this book, she explains issues she has encountered and had to overcome.

Sharetta is also a wife and mother of five children. The love for her children and grandchild has sparked a desire for her to become a more vocal advocate for abuse victims and their emotional healing.

AFFIRMATIONS AND ANTIDOTES

DEDICATION

To my children: Because of them, I have the strength and the determination to weather any storm. I love my "Fab Five": Elisha, Fredricka, Anderrious, Andravius, and Andriawna.

Sharetta

"TROUBLES DON'T LAST ALWAYS"

It is unrealistic to think that we will go through this life without challenges and obstacles. No one is immune. Life can sometimes throw us curve balls that will lead us to the valley of the shadow of death, but grace will help us get through it. "Troubles don't last always" is my empowering and motivating cliché. Not only is it cliché, it is also biblical. In 2 Corinthians 4:17, we learn that our afflictions are light and momentary. I also like the very familiar phrase, "This, too, shall pass." All of these things strengthen me when I am going through tough and trying times.

It took a while of growing and maturing for me to finally understand that troubles don't last always. For years, I could not see past my current situations. When I was imprisoned in the dungeon of sexual molestation, I could not see my deliverance. I hoped and prayed for a change, but I could not see the reality of that happening. I was living in the "now" with very little insight for the future. The twinkle and optimism that is sometimes visible in children's eyes had been dimmed by oppression and violation.

One person planted a glimmer of hope into my mind. Although she did not know my situation, the words she spoke were like oxygen to my suffocating soul. I adhered to her advice and within a matter of months, I was out of the dysfunction and into a new environment of peace. I was on my way to healing! Troubles don't last always!

When I was young mother and working in the fast-food industry, I could not see past the hamburgers I was assigned to make. The company I worked for had a color-coded system for dressing burgers: repeat white, red, and green twice. It was mayonnaise, ketchup, pickle, onion, tomato, and lettuce. I had become so indoctrinated with white, red, and green until I would dream about Christmas at night. There was no vision! I was robotic and operating routinely, much like a worker bee.

I had gone to college once but dropped out and forfeited a full academic scholarship. This was my second time around working at this same restaurant. The manager was a family friend. One day, he dropped a thought-seed into my psyche. He said, "My wife is a nurse. Have you ever thought of going to nursing school?" That seed germinated for approximately seven years before I graduated from a practical nursing program. About 14 years after the initial thought-seed, I graduated from a Registered Nursing program. Ten years later, I finished a Bachelor's program in Nursing. Troubles don't last always!

On July 26, 2010, I sat in a courtroom with my husband as he stood trial for possession of marijuana. We had been married for nine years, and the youngest of our five babies was to turn 10 years old in just two days. I had watched several people with equal or greater crimes walk out with fines and probation. I was naïve to the process and thought surely, my husband was coming back home with us (even though I was well aware the system was not fair). Eventually, the judge issues a sentence of 20 years, with 14 years suspended and six years to serve. I was devastated! Before the numbness of the shock could reach my feet, I left the courtroom and drove to a nearby church where I wept. It was difficult to see in that moment that there would be a light at the end of that tunnel; however, my husband only spent five months in a minimum-security facility. I picked him up on December 23rd—two days before Christmas. Troubles don't last always!

I shared these personal scenarios in my life to inform you that life for me has not been a crystal staircase. Not only do I have stories, but everyone has a story—sometimes more than one. Even if our lives were beds of roses, there would be thorns among them. That's just how life is. The Bible tells us that weeping may endure for a night, but joy comes in the morning. Sometimes, the time between the weeping and the joy seems long, lonely, and uncertain. The key is to remain occupied in the process!

AFFIRMATIONS AND ANTIDOTES

"HOW TO WAIT ON JOY"

We can't just sit and twiddle our thumbs while we wait for our troubles to pass. In the very popular 23rd Psalm, the Psalmist David said, "Yea, though I walk through the valley of the shadow of death..." Even though there was darkness in the valley, he remained in motion and in faith.

What do you do when you are going through? How do you wait on your situation to change?

Listed below are three things we SHOULDN'T do:

1. The number one thing we should not do is worry. We should not worry if we have a blessed assurance that this valley experience will not last forever. There is an old English Proverb that says, "Worrying is like sitting in a rocking chair: It gives you something to do but never gets you anywhere." Worrying is nonproductive, but it can leave health issues behind. Hypertension, stroke, and even gastric ulcers have been associated with worrying. It is tempting for us to believe that we can control all outcomes and to be overly-concerned about how; however, we do not own a sovereign stake in the matter. I believe that God is God and that He has my best interests at heart. The final verdict may not be the way I intend, but I rest in the sovereignty of God for my life.
2. Resting in God will also help us not to make erroneous emotion-based decisions. Find your filter for which every decision flows through. My filter is the Bible. Sometimes, the Bible does not agree with my emotions. What, then, should I follow: my emotions or the Word of God? I have had my share of collateral damage from following what I thought, felt, liked, or what someone else said

that sounded correct. At what point do we stop winning then losing because of our emotion-based decision-making skills?
3. Unprofitable decisions will lead to discouragement. Discouragement will lead to the desire to give up. Whatever you do, don't give up! Give up should never be an option. Through no's, naysayers, and negativities, we continue to stand—knowing that this, too, shall pass. There will always be lemons, but how refreshing is ice-cold lemonade? I have been at my wits end and thought about giving up. I've even thought life would be better without me in it. The enemy serves up all kinds of thoughts while you are having a wilderness experience. You have the power to remind him what is written about you and your identity. I love to recite from Deuteronomy: "I am the head and not the tail, far above and not beneath." That affirmation and many others have helped me get through tough times.

Learning to affirm yourself can help you as well. I have explained things that are nonproductive to us during hard times, but there are some powerful, productive, and positive things you can do that will help you get through. I have already named affirmations.

Another thing is meditation. Meditation is not spooky and mysterious. I'm talking about meditating on what you believe. I believe God, so I meditate on His Word. Sometimes, I add worship music during meditation, candles, and fragrances. Find the calming measures that work best for you.

Along with meditation comes prayer. Praying what God says avails much. God is so good in that He created a way through prayer that I could dump my concerns on Him and He would exchange them for something He has. I can give Him my ashes, and He will give me is beauty. I can give Him my tears, and He will give me His joy. He knew that we couldn't handle it alone, so He made a way to lighten our loads.

Journaling has lightened my load as well. Sometimes, my entries started by saying, "Dear God"—other times they haven't. My intentions were to leave my thoughts and tears on the paper to Him. From the altar of my heart, I wrote things that needed to be burned. When there was no one to talk to or when no one understood, journaling helped me to keep my wits about me.

Aside from the affirmations, meditations, prayers, and journaling, an ounce of prevention is worth a pound of cure. We should change our mindsets to become more proactive instead of reactive. There's a parable in the Bible about two men who were building a house. The wise man took the extra time and effort to make sure the foundation of the house was strong and sturdy. The other man did not. They both experienced the same torrential rains and winds. The wise man experienced less damage because of his foundation.

Needless to say, we will face the same issues. The foundation that we choose to use will lessen our blow. Our damage from the rains and winds will be lessened. Make sure that you are as proactive as possible so that you experience less of a blow as possible. Troubles don't last always!

Betty Speaks is the Executive Director of Strap Em Up Boot Camp and the Founder of Betty Speaks "IT". As a Certified Life Coach, Betty specializes in Intentional Transformation as well as LIFE Restoration. She is an Army Veteran, Ambassador to The Veteran Woman, LLC, a Global Network Virtual Marketer, a serial Entrepreneur, Four-Time Best-Selling Author, Ordained Pastor, Jesus Woman Coordinator for the State of South Carolina for Godheads Ministry, Ambassador to the Pink Pulpit Ministry, a Designated Mastery Story-Teller, and a Life Group Leader at Redemption Worldwide Outreach Ministry.

Betty holds a Bachelor of Science in Business Management from the University of Maryland. She is pursuing her Doctoral in Theology. She received five Outstanding Businesswoman of the Year Awards from the American Business Women's Association.

Betty Speaks passion and her LIFE'S calling is to help others not just survive their 'IT", but thrive through their "IT" while encountering LIFE's chances, changes, and challenges.

AFFIRMATIONS AND ANTIDOTES

Betty Speaks is the Executive Director at Strap Em Up Boot Camp and the Founder of Betty Speaks "IT", As a Certified Life Coach, Betty specializes in Intentional Transformation, as well LIFE restoration.

She is an Army Veteran, Ambassador to The Veteran Woman LLC., a Global Network Virtual Marketer a serial Entrepreneur, 4x Best Selling Author, Ordained Pastor, Jesus Woman Coordinator for the State of South Carolina for Godheads Ministry, Ambassador to the Pink Pulpit Ministry, a Designated Mastery Story Teller and a Life Group Leader at Redemption Worldwide Outreach Ministry.

Betty holds a Bachelor of Science in Business Management from the University of Maryland. She is pursuing her Doctoral in Theology. She received 5 Outstanding Businesswoman of The Year awards from the American Business Women's Association. Betty Speaks passion and LIFE's calling is to help others not just survive their "IT" but thrive through their "IT" while encountering LIFEs chances, changes and challenges.

DEDICATION

As always, I give honor to God for His presence in my life, and to a special person whom He has blessed into my life; A phenomenally phenomenal woman who answered His call, Dr. Marilyn Porter. She truly has a prevailing testimony as it is written regarding how the Lord our God *"Gives strength to the weary and increases the power of the weak. Isaiah 40:29"!*

Betty

AFFIRMATIONS AND ANTIDOTES

His Presence Comforts ME

When I think of affirmations that strengthens me, I think about what comes naturally and easy for me conquer. I don't select characteristics that I would like to partake or that I regard. As, this would seem a bit to deceptive towards the genuine calling on my life. I especially avoid those affirmations that appear as a weakness for me. Meaning if I can't dance in the rain, why bother.

Yet, I intentionally choose those affirmations that strengthens me. The affirmations that are connected to my core. What is so noticeable is that I almost don't notice what it is that strengthens me because, they are personal and hidden within mine inner being forevermore, especially, since they have become my very nature. Also, my strengths possess a uniqueness of who I am according to His Purpose for my Life. Knowing that the presence of the Lord is my uttermost reinforcement.

For the most part, I felt extremely grateful, once I embraced the memories of my life journey. Ideally, the presence of the Lord my God and His provision throughout my life has given me gratification, appreciation and strength. I personally recognized that I did the best I could at any given time throughout my life and now I am equipped to Let Go of those things I cannot control, and Let God perform His blessings accordingly. His word has empowered me with a clear vision of my next endeavors in life especially as I continue to Live Intentionally for Eternity (LIFE) for His Kingdom.

Affirmation: I shall be still and wait upon the Lord Exodus 14:14 NIV

Antidote: Affirming that I will not fight my own battle. I will allow the Lord to accomplish His deliverance each time I encounter a satanic attack. As it is written in the book of Exodus [13] *Moses answered the people, "Do not be*

afraid. Stand firm and you will see the deliverance the LORD will bring you today. The Egyptians you see today you will never see again. ¹⁴ The LORD will fight for you; you need only to be still." (NIV)

Reminds me that: *"they that wait upon the Lord shall renew their strength".* (Is. 40:31).

The minute you wait upon the Lord, are you strengthened in Him your mind will not be filled with curiosity and uncertainties. Once we stop and wait upon our Lord, our hearts will be filled with confidence.

Should one find that their waiting leads them into discouragement and hopelessness, then they are waiting on a situation or perhaps an individual rather than the Lord. Waiting on the situation or even an individual may lead one into frustration and doubt, nevertheless when we as believers wait upon the Lord our heart is filled with contentment, hope, and peace.

The devil gets extremely upset when we stand still and wait upon our Lord through fasting, prayer, worship and especially meditation.

Affirmation: I shall take everything to Him in Prayer and Petition!

"Do not be anxious about anything, but in every situation, by prayer and petition, with thanksgiving, present your requests to God Philippians 4:6 (NIV)."

Leaning upon this verse has been such a life change my life. A few years back, my husband and I were enthusiastic about relocating from his job in New England and claiming new roots in South Carolina. But then again, the unknowns and unexpected challenges left me feeling somewhat anxious. The thoughts of sorting and packing up possessions. Looking for a place to live.

AFFIRMATIONS AND ANTIDOTES

My finding or establishing new relations. Making my way from place to place in a new city, in addition to getting settled. It was all . . . alarming. As I thought about my things "to-do" list, words written by the apostle Paul resonated in my mind; Don't worry but pray (Phil. 4:6–7).

Antidote: Affirming the recollection of Paul's letter to the Philippian church, identifying just how he empowered his friends who were facing unknown situations as did he, then telling them, "Do not be anxious about anything, but in every situation, by prayer and petition, with thanksgiving, present your requests to God" (Phil 4:6). You see Paul was shipwrecked, he was horribly beaten, and he was imprisoned. This was revelation to the unknown and had to be very challenging yet relevant of one feeling the emotions anxiety to that which was unforeseen.

However, Paul's words are breathtaking and filled with reassurance. Primarily, life is not deprived of uncertainties; when it derived in the form of a significant life change, family matters, financial issues or health concerns. What I continue to learn is that God cares. He invites us to let go of our fears of the unforeseen by giving them to Him. When we do, He, who knows all things, promises that His peace, "which transcends all understanding, will guard" our heart and mind in Christ Jesus (Phil 4:7).

Reminds me that: Philippian chapter four expresses the wonderful resource of prayers and how in prayer we can take our anxieties to our Heavenly Father and discover His well-being and harmony while enjoying His Presence. Nevertheless, in the verses prior Paul's prayer was a reminder. In fact, Paul gives us additional reasons to substitute anxiety with trust. Also, Paul says, "Let your gentleness be evident to all. The Lord is near" (Phil 4:5). Essentially, each of us have the promise of God's closeness to quiet our fears. In every single situation, our

God allows us to face while on our LIFE journey, His presence and experience His provision.

His Presence shall strengthen me. Knowing that He will place me in situations that only He can bring me out of because my life is not my own especially since I have given myself to my Lord and savior Jesus Christ.

Prayer: Dearest Heavenly Father, it is such a lovely blessing knowing that we as your children never ever have to be anxious about whatever we may encounter! Thank you, Heavenly father, for reminding us that we can come to You and express to You our genuine matters and then we just stand still in your presence. We thank you dear Father for the reminder of Paul and his strength knowing that he had faith in you and your presence throughout his challenging unforeseen encounters. Thank You repeatedly for who You are and what You are doing in our lives and the lives of our family, friends and coworkers. Blessings be unto you forevermore Amen.

Action Taker: Father grant me the serenity to accept the things I cannot change, the courage to change the things I can, and the wisdom to know the difference. Strengthen me to live in the presence rather than being anxious about my future. Remind me to stand still and wait doing challenging encounters. Father, should my mind wonder to things that it shouldn't please bring me back to realization or reality. Deliver me from anxiety and increase my faith in YOU.

AFFIRMATIONS AND ANTIDOTES

Tshcanna M. Taylor, MBA—affectionately called "The Purpose Engineer"—is a Certified Life Solutionist, Best-Selling Author, Speaker, and Entrepreneur.

A huge advocate for women walking authentically in their purpose, Tschanna is a change agent and revolutionary dedicated to elevating women to redefine, reaffirm, and rebuild their life's mess into a masterpiece.

Tschanna uses her testimony of faith to share her own personal story of childhood/domestic violence, infidelity, and a traumatic near-death experience as the catalyst of her teachings.

True to her calling, she is a real, purpose-driven woman!

DEDICATION

I would like to dedicate my story to every reader who has ever encountered defeat. Just know that you ARE NOT defeated.

Tshcanna

AFFIRMATIONS AND ANTIDOTES

I overcome fears because through every trial and test, God gives me the strength to endure.

Use your struggles to redefine you:
"For I know the plans I have for you, declares the LORD; plans for good and not evil, to give you a future and a hope."
Jeremiah 29:11, TLB

Use your struggles to reaffirm your faith:
"Yet what we suffer now is nothing compared to the glory He will give us later."
Romans 8:18, TLB

Use your struggles to rebuild your life on purpose:
"Once again, I will rebuild you. Once again, you will take up your tambourines and dance joyfully."
Jeremiah 31:4, GNT

Use your struggles to renew:
"Therefore, if anyone is in Christ, he is a new creation. The old has passed away; behold, the new has come."
2 Corinthians 5:17, ESV

Strengthens ME:
No matter what obstacle I face, I already have the victory over every test, every struggle, every problem, every obstacle, and every situation.

"Because of the routines we follow, we often forget that life is an ongoing adventure."
~ Maya Angelou ~

When I hear the word 'strength', the first thing that comes to mind is someone at their local gym, training to life 100-pound weights. But real strength? It doesn't come from kettlebells and bench presses; it comes from within. It's displayed during the trials we endure and the issues we face. True strength is a gift from God.

Do you ever feel like you're waiting for life to happen for you? Do you ever feel that your daily routines keep you stuck while there's something you know you are purposed to do, but a silent "can't" stops you? You may see a bolder, brighter future for yourself, but when you look at your current state, your strength fades. You give up before even starting, yet you remain hopeful or prayerful that change is going to come. There has to be a better way, right?

Instead of trusting God through the process, we tiptoe to the edge or stick our big toe in the water for a temperature check. Whatever the reason, we put off taking the big leap. One day stacks on another and, as time runs away from us, we sit around with the "shoulda-woulda-couldas". Why? Because we are afraid we don't have the strength to make it.

I struggled with a decision to leave a mentally and verbally abusive marriage. I was married to a Deacon who was 13 years my senior. The marriage started out great, but gradually changed over time. There was no intimacy and no affection. In their place, there was plenty of verbal and mental abuse. To the church we attended, he thought that to the people, we were the power couple in the church. That was until one day, a church member told me that I appeared unhappy and that she was there for me if I wanted to talk.

Most of his issues were not being able to separate work from home. Whenever there was an issue at work, my day went straight to hell. He took a lot of his frustrations out on me. Even being intimate was forceful. I was drained emotionally, spiritually, verbally, and mentally. The marriage was so bad, I felt it was necessary to take my own life, just so I wouldn't be with him any longer.

I remember sitting in the driveway one evening after work for over an hour, trying to decide should I go in the house or drive off...never to return.

Although he wasn't physically abusive, mental and verbal abuse exchanged places with the physical. I walked in to talk to him about marital counseling with hopes he was willing to put forth the same effort as me. Instead, he accused me of cheating and made it clear that if couldn't have me, no one else would.

I never thought in a million years that the man who made a vow before God and our family to love and protect me would pull a rifle on me. To make matters worse, He decided to scare me further by surprising me with his new purchase of a boa constrictor. I held my breath, all while trying to figure out: When did the Deacon get a snake? Lord, what do I do now?

At that point, there was nothing more to "work out". I was out of there!

I left to stay at a friend's house as I prepared for work the next morning. While on lunch, I went to the restroom, still trying to grasp the previous night's events. In disbelief, I stared at my reflection in the mirror while wondering: How did I get here? Then, a woman came out of the bathroom stall and started speaking to herself saying, "Okay. I'll do it." I looked around to see who else was in the bathroom with us, but it was just us. She then began to share a Word from God specifically for me. As she began speaking, I knew instantly that she was God-sent. There was no way she knew major details of my marriage. I had never seen her before at work—and I had been on the job for four years!

She said, "God is going to provide you a way of escape. God told you to get out of this situation once before but you stayed, trying to make the marriage work. You didn't wait on God's answer when you prayed about him. God will never leave you nor forsake you, regardless of the decisions you make. This time, God will give you another escape plan but you must act quickly because if you wait, you may not live to tell about it." I thanked the Woman of God for her obedience by sharing God's specific word for me.

Fear left me after receiving another confirmation from my grandmother the next day. A week after this incident, I emptied the entire house. I told you earlier: I was outta there! God did NOT need to tell me to go a third time!

I was proud of myself for pushing past fear. There were many times I wanted to leave but was too afraid to do so. I went through a lot during the legal separation and divorce. He found out where I lived and tormented me daily, even throwing rocks at my bedroom window. I filed for a restraining order, thinking that would stop him. It didn't. The police didn't do much to protect and serve me.

Once he saw that I was no longer afraid of him, he left a voicemail to tell me he didn't want me anyway and that all he wanted me for was my sex and my money in the first place. He had some nerve! He wasn't quite the

AFFIRMATIONS AND ANTIDOTES

"looker" in the first place...but I digress. The tormenting stopped and I eventually regained my peace.

It took a lot of prayer, fasting, meditating, and counseling to gain the strength to heal. Things that should have never happened did, leaving me in a cemented place. It appeared my life was spiraling out of control. Through this experience, I realized I am an overcomer.

Grandma always told me, "If you live long enough, life will test you. If you don't obtain strength, the pressures of life will break you. Love yourself enough to get back up when you are knocked down. Never give up when all looks lost. Muster the willpower, resilience, and faith to get back in the game of life. Strength will help you withstand life's stresses, challenges, and catastrophes."

Life can be hard. Lord knows; I have the scars to prove it. But for you I say: Let go of any past hurts and focus on your future. Change begins when you redirect your thoughts and actions towards what you want. With God's help, you will gain the strength you need to push through this test. Life begins when we summon the strength to do what we are afraid of. This could be learning how to plan events, going back to school, writing a book, starting a business, or making a hard decision.

It doesn't mean you may not stumble and fall or that you slow down to catch your breath, but whatever you do, heal, redefine, reaffirm, rebuild, and renew, moving forward in God's way. You are strong and your faith in the Lord fuels that strength. Together, you and God will accomplish so much. Indeed, you are capable of overcoming.

To everything, there is a season and time. Today might have you down. You may not want to get out of the bed. This week may have seemed impossible to make it through. This year may have started off wrong for you. Whatever your stage in life, acknowledge where you are by recognizing your season, release your fears to Jesus, and reach your goals one step at a time. These obstacles will graduate in time.

You are an overcomer!

AFFIRMATIONS AND ANTIDOTES

Shellie Sandys is from Wiltshire in the United Kingdom. She is the Founder and CEO of CrystalConfidence.uk and SpiritBound.co.uk. Shellie has been practicing spiritual connection since 2006. She is a loving and devoted Mum of two beautiful children and Wife to her forever soulmate.

Throughout the last 12 years, Shellie has grown with confidence and strength by overcoming fears and struggles both mentally and physically. She is now living a Free-Spirit lifestyle and helps others do the same.

I am full of strength and courage to get through these tough times.

I am positive that all good things will come to me at exactly the right time.

I will overcome any obstacle that gets in my way.

I am powerful, beautiful, and whole.

I am in control of my body and mind.

This will go away. It's not the final destination.

This is not real. This is just my mind playing tricks on me.

Anxiety does not rule my life. I RULE MY LIFE!

These words have been repeated more times than I can remember. Throughout the past, I have always been a strong, independent woman, but sometimes when you feel like the world comes crashing down on you, it can quite literally knock you right back down to the floor!

It was a normal winter's day. The sun was shining down onto my car as I was driving along the open road, singing along to the music on the radio and looking forward to getting errands done. I was laughing with my son, Tyler, as we were lifting each other up after a tough time with his health when all of a sudden, my body started to feel ever-so-different. I could feel myself not being present properly as I started to deteriorate as I was driving along. I had nowhere to pull over and was trying to shake off whatever was happening to me. Shortly after, I had a heavy feeling in my head and my left eye started to lose sight. I started to get super-scared, as I had no idea what

AFFIRMATIONS AND ANTIDOTES

was happening to me. I had to try my best to stay positive and strong for Tyler who was seated right beside me.

I saw a pull-in up ahead and was aiming for it, when suddenly the traffic light turned red—just as I was about to pull in. At this point, I could barely recognize anything around me or even sense that my hands were my hands. It was a horrible feeling and quite difficult to explain.

I was waiting at the traffic light and asked Tyler to call someone...anyone! I couldn't get my words out properly. I couldn't lift myself to press anything or focus clearly. My sight started to go all black and white. No color could be seen. Then, everything started to disappear altogether.

I am not sure how I made it off the road but I did. I am truly grateful for my guidance to safety for myself and my son.

Scared for my life, I stayed put with Tyler helping me by talking to me and reminding me that I am strong and that someone was on the way. He was only 10 years old at the time and so brave! If he wasn't in the car that day, things might have been different but I know that he was meant to be off that day.

This event left me mentally drained for months on end, not knowing truly why such a thing would happen to me—until I came to the conclusion that it was a lesson to strengthen me even more than ever before and to put me on the right path—the path that is now my passion for helping others overcome anything that knocks them down mentally.

How I grew from the experience was not easy. I had lots of doctors, support, and guidance from everyone around me. Most of all, being able to heal spiritually was a powerful tool! After being left with severe anxiety from the incident, it was time to heal and grow with inner-strength.

How to Strengthen You

You need rest. Rest is key to grow with strength. The body must heal and recharge. If you are overcoming something and you're going every single day without time for yourself, this will eventually destroy you. Listen to your body, as it knows what is best for you. I truly mean that: It's necessary!

Talk to YOURSELF. If there is a situation that you cannot control or is too overwhelming to think about, speak to yourself. What would you say to someone in your situation? Now, tell yourself that exact advice and believe it 100%. It will help you.

Do things that scare you that are new to you. One way I have found that helps strengthen me is to push myself out of the usual routine. Doing the same thing day in and day out is not good for anyone. Start a new hobby. Go for walks. Stand in the rain. Do yoga. Journal. Go and have a coffee on your own. Start small, then you will feel yourself get stronger every single day.

Ask for help or advice. When we feel vulnerable, we feel alone. That's no way to feel. Remember: There is always someone out there to help you. Even if you don't know anyone, there will be someone waiting to offer advice. Don't be alone. Speak up! This alone is one of the main things that will help strengthen you.

Meditation. This isn't for everyone, but if I didn't put it down, I wouldn't be sharing all that has helped ME grow with strength to take on my dreams and become a new and improved version of myself.

AFFIRMATIONS AND ANTIDOTES

Silence the mind at least once every single day. Check in with how you are feeling and what mood you are in at that exact moment in time. This is great if you're not in the right mood for what you are doing. You can instantly flip your mood from nervous, anxious, or scared to positive, happy, and excited within seconds. How, you ask?

Silence your mind by taking a few deep breaths. Feel your whole body in tune. Now, think about how you feel right now in this moment. Is it how you want to feel or would you like to change it? If you want to change your mood, simply ask for the unwanted feelings to be taken away. Ask to be filled with the feelings you desire. Feel the movement and the light as you are filling yourself up with love, light, and happiness.

Guided meditations are also amazing in order to create a better day for you. There are many on YouTube.

Journaling. My last antidote for building your strength is to buy yourself a new notebook or journal and start writing down how your day is going. This doesn't have to be lengthy or perfect; this is just a way to get all the negativity out of your head and onto paper, leaving room for new, more positive energy and thoughts to come to you. Once it's out of your mind, you will feel lighter and free of worry. Write down what you are good at and what you love to do. Focus on these things when moving forward in life, as doing what you love will always win!

Remember: You are STRONGER than you think. All the STRENGTH you need is within you. You CAN and WILL access all the strength you need. You just need to believe that it's there and for you to use.

Stay true! Be YOU!

Gemma Gilfoyle is a Life Coach, Entrepreneur, Speaker, and Influencer. She has had businesses since 2010 and is all about EMPOWERING and UPLIFTING people by getting them to step into their POWER. She is a Mum of two children and lives in Liverpool, United Kingdom.

AFFIRMATIONS AND ANTIDOTES

DEDICATION

I dedicate this to my two boys who have made me who I am. I love and cherish each moment with them.

Gemma

Strength Affirmations:

I am strong, confident, and worthy.

I am healthy, grateful, and unique.

I am happy. I am me!

Strength and Virtue:
Find your inner-strength and build on it!

You truly don't realize how strong you are. How many times have you been pushed to your limit by your family, friends, partner, kids, health issues, or even your work colleagues? How many times have you said, "That's it! I can't do this anymore?" or "I am not strong enough!" or "I quit!" or "I have had enough!" Yet every day, we continue on our path. We know that we must do it because no one else will. You are STRONG, BEAUTIFUL, and CONFIDENT. Embrace it!

Becoming a single young mum at 17 years old and then being diagnosed with anxiety and depression was one of the toughest fights I have had to go through. I knew that for the rest of my life, I was going to have to fight every day—not only to protect my mental health but also to make sure my son would not suffer while I tried to deal with my conditions.

The big problem came when the doctors said the only thing they would do was offer counseling. Now, while I am not against it, the experience I had with the counselor was not good. I was actually left feeling worse and believing I was at fault. I had two choices: I could either just let everything dissolve and give up OR dig deep, push through, and give my child everything I possibly could.

AFFIRMATIONS AND ANTIDOTES

I decided that because my mum was already helping me with my son (she was and still is incredible), I would just keep going forward and try to forget it. What really pushed me to keep moving forward was my son and knowing he depended on me for everything. If I didn't provide what he needed, he would have gone without.

I had to find the strength to get up every day (even when I didn't want to) to work and provide for my son. I found the strength to put one foot in front of the other and never give up, just so my son never went without. My anxiety and depression never went away; they were always there. However, I chose to push through...for my son.

In February 2015, I knew I needed to get help. I was finally ready to think of me and take back my life.

My son had become a strong, independent teenager. I had held it together for too long. That day was the day I took control of my life and started to build on my inner-strength. I would NO longer let my mental health dictate who I was and what I wanted to achieve.

"Don't let your past define who you are. It has given you the strength and wisdom you have today."

In October 2016, 16 years after giving birth to my first child, I gave birth to my second child. This time, my life was changed for different reasons. I knew I had done my best for my firstborn, especially being a single mum, but I wanted more for my children. I knew that I missed a lot the first time around and did not and would not allow that to happen again.

Again, I found myself having to dig deep and find the strength to deal with so many changes with myself and within my life. This was a strength I never knew existed. I don't think anyone really does until they are tested. You always think you can't handle any more, yet without realizing it, you continue—always pushing through and keeping everything together.

I fight each day to control my mind and body. This is a battle I will have for the rest of my life, but guess what? That battle gets easier and easier each and every day. I never knew that by getting help and taking those first steps, they would set me on my journey to help other people do the same.

Do you ever feel like you're here for something bigger than yourself but don't know what that "it" is? That's because you are! You are a person. YOU were born to live this LIFE, so DO IT!

This lasts year has been my biggest growth in my strength. By just accepting myself as I am, I have learned that we are all human and cannot be everything to everyone. Just because you cry, it does not make you weak. In fact, by crying, it shows your strength! It gives you a release—a way to let go, clear your mind, and start again.

I have always known I am here for something bigger than myself (much like you are feeling right now). It also took me a long time to do something with it. Why? Because I needed to experience certain things in order to be able to step into my purpose to give value and impact to each person I reach.

I always knew I was here to help and serve people who struggle. I had done the work for 11 years within my previous job. Still, finding my purpose made me STRONG. It cemented into me that all my struggles were for a reason: To be able to show and share with you that your strength comes from within yourself!

AFFIRMATIONS AND ANTIDOTES

Building on yourself daily will see your inner-strength grow. Be grateful and gain control of your thoughts and feelings every day. Your heart and mind are your most precious possessions, so take care of them and help them heal. Most of all, just remember:

YOU ARE ENOUGH.

YOU ARE STRENGTH.

YOU ARE AN INCREDIBLE, UNIQUE, AND INSPIRING PERSON WHO HAS SO MUCH TO GIVE!

Rebecca Adams is a Life Mastery Expert specializing in Mindset. She is a Life and Business Coach, International Best-Selling Co-Author, Entrepreneur, and Influencer. She has had businesses since 2003 and she EMPOWERS people to FEEL ALIVE and live a PHENOMENAL life.

Rebecca focuses on Impact and Value and her highest ability is to see the positive in any negative situation and change people's MINDSET into more positive, productive thinking by motivating and empowering them to concentrate on their own personal development and gratitude daily.

Her lifetime philosophy is: "You CAN and WILL achieve anything you set your mind to."

Her lifetime mantra is: "Keep going…ALWAYS."

Rebecca is a Mum of two, of which her son has special needs. She is also a British Army Veteran and lives in Wiltshire, United Kingdom.

AFFIRMATIONS AND ANTIDOTES

Affirmations That Strengthen Me

Healing Affirmations

I am powerful and confident.

I am so strong, nothing can knock me down.

I am my own superhero.

Healing Virtue

You are never given an obstacle that you can't deal with and overcome. You must remember that you are a strong and powerful human being who can deal with anything that is thrown your way. No matter how tragic or heartbreaking, you CAN get through it—even by taking small steps each and every day. Allow your mind to believe it, see it, and then...GO FOR IT!

As parents, we have to be strong for our children. The one word that comes to mind is PROTECTION. We have to protect our children from anything that we feel and deem to be harmful but still give them their own wings to fly. We have to allow our children the freedom to make their own mistakes and learn from them. Allow the to explore the world, achieve their dreams, and be happy. As well, teach them that it is okay to cry and be sad sometimes.

I want to share with you my 2011/2012 story that I don't share publicly. STRENGTH is the word that summarizes everything to do with the life-changing, monumental tragedy that happened all those years ago. It's a story of STRENGTH, COURAGE, HOPE, and RELENTLESS DRIVE to KEEP GOING ALWAYS—no matter what!

My husband and I were divorced back in 2005. After he left the military in 2006, he applied for a job in America with an oil company. He was loving life—skydiving, working, traveling, and exploring the world.

In October 2011, I received a message out of the blue one day on Facebook from a friend of his. The message stated that Ryan had gone missing and hadn't shown up for work. This actually didn't make sense, as he had always wanted to live and work in America. He had his whole life and career ahead of him.

AFFIRMATIONS AND ANTIDOTES

I contacted his family straight away and wanted to share all the details that I knew from what his friend had told me. Sure enough, Ryan had gone missing! No one knew where he was at all. So, our mission to find him began on that day.

His cousin set up a Facebook group, and we all added everyone we knew to the group. We had a poster made by another of his friends and distributed it all around social media—anywhere and everywhere. I gained access to the sheriffs in the state he had gone missing from and got up-to-date information from them, too. I also updated everyone in the group and family members. All the while, I had not told my children anything.

At the time, I was running my business from home, taking my daughter to and from school each day, and helping my special needs son. Life got hectic very quickly. Emails, messages, and phone calls were going back and forth from all around the world. I was staying up late to talk with my contacts in America, as they were six hours behind the United Kingdom.

We had posters made that were printed and put in truckers' vehicles and distributed everywhere. It was kind of difficult to find someone who has gone missing from thousands of miles across the ocean. I contacted every organization in the United Kingdom to see if they could help. Ryan was added to the Missing Person's database, and I was solidly relentless in my search day in and day out.

I did a timeline from where Ryan had gone missing to where the sheriff said was the last sighting of him. I tracked his mobile phone and credit card, all while trying not to cry or get upset as I ran my business, cooked for my children, did the daily school run, and everything else. All I wanted was to find Ryan.

We were told that Ryan had just disappeared and that his pajamas were folded up neatly on his bed (something that Ryan never ever did...and I've known him since I was 16 years old). There were lots of other things that just didn't make any sense.

I had a horrible feeling every single day from October 11th, 2011. I didn't know why I was losing weight. I was crying and sad but all the while, I had to stay strong because I had my children. I would still do my work, and my clients had no idea what was going on. Neither did my neighbors or school teachers. Bonfire Night on November 5th came and went. Christmas passed by, too. We still had not heard anything and continued to work tirelessly to find Ryan. I raised a glass for him as the New Year approached. Still nothing!

Where was he? Why wasn't he getting in contact with anyone?

I called in so many favors from people I knew in the military and to anyone who had family in America to see if they could help at all. The days kept passing by. I kept updating the days in the Facebook group. Day 25...Day 50...Day 89...etc. Every day, I used to look for a rainbow and would smile when I saw one. That was HOPE to me.

Our wedding anniversary passed (January 5th) and even though we were divorced, the piece of paper didn't mean anything—at least not at that time. I was relentless with my pursuit to find Ryan, regardless of how long it took. I had an obligation to find him. You know something? Tragedy sometimes creeps up on you without you even knowing or having a glimpse.

On Day 96, I received a Facebook message from a lady in California who told me to call her. I did and got through to a receptionist who couldn't pass me to the lady, as she needed to know what department she was with. I messaged the lady back on Facebook and received a message within five minutes telling me the department she was with: It was the Coroner's Department...and she was the Coroner! I stood there staring at those words for what felt like forever.

I phoned the number again and spoke to the Coroner who told me that she had a John Doe, had found the Facebook group, and contacted me directly, as I was his ex-wife and the driving force of the whole mission. I collapsed on the kitchen floor in tears. She had to be wrong! California? Ryan couldn't be there! He had gone missing in TEXAS!

I made notes of what she needed me to do and then I phoned Ryan's stepdad to inform him. I also had to phone Ryan's sister. It was a very sad day for us all. We decided not to tell anyone else (not even those in the Facebook group) until the next day. We needed time for us and for the news to sink in.

Day 97, I posted in the Facebook group. It was sad writing those words. Then came the biggest job for me: I had to tell my children!

Have you ever been in a situation whereby you had to be your STRONGEST at your most WEAKEST moment?

My friend Julie said that she'd be there with me every step of the way when I told the children. So, I chose February half-term to tell them. Because my son has special needs, I decided to tell my daughter first. She was eight years old at the time. It was the most painful thing I have ever had to do. Where my courage and strength came from, I have no idea. I knew that could do it. I had to.

With my son, I had to do things differently. I decided to show him a photo of Ryan and then go on to explain in ways that my son would understand. I set up counseling for my daughter at school.

Then came the process of identifying Ryan and raising money to bring him home to repatriate him. We failed to raise the money required, so he had to be cremated. The list goes on and on.

When tragedy strikes, you don't know how you're going to cope until you're in the moment. You can't prepare for those types of things. All you can do is step into your power and be a tower of strength for you and the people around you. You have a choice: Will it make you or break you?

Remember: You are stronger than you think and you are never given anything you can't handle. You are unstoppable in many ways, much like I was during my journey. I made it my non-negotiable mission to find Ryan. I never stopped, no matter how tired or upset I was.

Know that crying is a sign of strength, not weakness. You ARE strong. Nothing can knock you down if you don't allow it to. Move those mountains and become your own superhero!

AFFIRMATIONS AND ANTIDOTES

Jessica Schuurman is Editor of Three-Time #1 Best-Selling book, The Unstoppable Woman of Purpose"; Co-Author of #1 Best-Selling book, Affirmations and Antidotes That Heal Me; Freelancing Writer; Editor; and Black Sheep Weirdo Visionary who seeks to unleash your meaning and God-given purpose through His Word alone, teaching others how to live life righteously.

The Book of Psalms.

In the Book of Psalms, King David shows his anger, confusion, and praise in the Lord. King David was just a man blessed by God's hand. He lived out his purpose that God set for him.

Strength needs to come from a place within. It needs to be given fuel on a daily basis, and your strength needs an ultimate purpose. So, what gives you strength? How do you accumulate your strength? Why do you need strength?

Maybe you're thinking that everyone needs strength just to make it through the day. There is this thing to remember: To need strength is to push forward out of the comfortable and into the uncomfortable. This is where you will gain lasting change. A lot of the time, being uncomfortable is such an unpleasant feeling that people tend to give up before they receive their reward of joy and pleasure.

Strength keeps you going when things get tough, when you don't want to get up at 5:00 a.m., or make your bed before the day begins. Strength is a necessity to have in order to keep consistency and to help yourself become the best version of you!

So, how do we fuel our strength? Well, fueling your strength is the same as fueling your faith. Jesus came and died for our sins so that we could be free in this fallen world—free to choose God's purpose for our lives, having faith that God's promises will come to full fruition and aid in giving you strength to press on.

Faith = Spiritual

Strength = Physical

AFFIRMATIONS AND ANTIDOTES

Together, they are the same concept. You need one to fuel the other.

Now, I want you think about WHY you need strength. Isn't your life good enough? Could you live like this forever? Are you happy with who you are and where you have come? If your children were where you are, would you be content with that?

Ultimately, you need a WHY. Why are you getting up every day and making your bed? Why are you staying up until 4:00 a.m. to work on an assignment?

You could be thinking that the answer is God's promise to you...the outcome of your efforts. It is much greater than that. Usually, it's because of your children, you want a better life, or you want to show people who have had similar adversities that they, too, can do it. So, why do you need the strength in order to fulfill God's promise for you?

For me, the Book of Psalms is my strength, knowing that King David was just a man like any other who faced affliction. He speaks about his enemies and how he just wants God's protection. My strength is fueled by Psalms because I know that I am no better than anyone else. Just like a KING, I only ask for protection and guidance from Jesus, allowing me to fully surrender and allow His mighty works to flow through me.

In order to enable a strength inside of you, you have to admit to yourself that you are weak. This can be one of the most devastating things a person can do. Crushing your pride and ego all at the same time will, as a matter of fact, strengthen you to your core. Who is mightier than God Himself? No one! So, by surrendering to His love and might for you, you will allow Him to work through you in your life. Things that may have taken a complete toll on you by bringing you to your knees will no longer cause havoc. Circumstances that you would have never through possible for you to conquer will pass with flying colors. Surrendering is key.

Now, the real question is: How do I know what God wants to do in my life once I have given myself to Him? Well, the simple answer for this is PRAYER. I know when I was first looking for strength to achieve my goals, I thought prayer was praying over the rosary. I was raised Roman Catholic and that was all I knew. As I grew in my faith, I realized that Jesus wants nothing more than a real relationship with us. He wants us to tell Him everything, ask for help when we need it, and cast our worries on Him. Essentially, He wants to be our Life Source.

The way I started to do this was by journaling. No, not like 'Dear Dumb Diary'. I would sit there and talk to God. I would ask for forgiveness for all the sinful acts I had partaken in since the last time I prayed and then I would say, "Jesus, write through me today. Whatever you have to tell me, help guide me. Please write through me." If I had specific questions, I would ask them as well. Then, I waited until I felt the Holy Spirit flow through me and write whatever He had to say.

Most times, before I journal, I read the Psalms aloud. Have you ever heard of the saying, "Be still, my soul", in the Bible? Well, this is the perfect way to still your soul. Once you are comprehending everything that is being read and all your focus is on the Word, that is when you start to journal.

I want to share a story with you about the strength God gave me to pursue His purpose for my life. Simply stated: It was the hardest decision I ever had to make and follow through with.

AFFIRMATIONS AND ANTIDOTES

It had been months since I had last seen my fiancé (in the spirit, I mean). He had become this evil person, and every time I would say something he didn't like, he would come back and say something so mean to put me down. It was becoming a toxic environment. We couldn't say anything to each other without venom being spewed. I prayed and prayed, asking Jesus what to do. I counseled with others and they all told me it wasn't time to leave. Then, one day I prayed and Jesus told me it was time for me to leave this mess and create a new life. He assured me that this separation from the man I loved was only temporary. This effort was going to make our family new again.

I was so angry at the time, when I felt Jesus tell me to leave, I felt relief. I couldn't wait to get out and be free from the person I had become and the family we grew to be. My son deserved better. I knew that. I loved my fiancé. I knew that, too. Once the time came and the arrangements were made for my son and me to leave, I had to tell my fiancé. I forced the words out of me. I truly believe every word that came out of my mouth was Jesus speaking.

Confrontation was never my strong suit. Then, the reasons I was leaving just disappeared and it seemed like nothing bad had even happened. For a second, I was weak and thought that I would stay, but then the Holy Spirit came and convicted me. It was the craziest thing. The second I said I would stay, it started up again. The next day, I decided I was going to leave. When I thought about all the things I had to do—preparing to leave, packing our things, and living like a stranger in my own home—it's a memory that is faded. I know that I was not in control of making my move happen. My admitting I was weak and letting "Jesus take the wheel" allowed me to step into the new life He had created for me and my family. Right now, I am still in the process of receiving all that Jesus has for me, but without His mighty strength, I wouldn't be able to keep going and press on.

Journaling gives me the comfort and strength I need to keep going into a valley of the unknown. My 'why' is my son: to be able to give him a life of comfort, a standard for living, and the knowledge of how to obtain it himself. In achieving my goal, there will be more to come. This life is a never-ending lesson, preparing us for what Jesus has in store for us in Heaven.

Your strength is within you. You just need to have faith that it's there and that Jesus is capable of completing it through you. You have to surrender, and all of your questions will be answered by the Almighty Jesus Christ.

"For God so loved the world, that He gave His only Begotten Son; that whosoever believeth in Him should not perish, but have everlasting life."
John 3:16

My prayer for you is that my chapter helps you lean on the Lord. May you be strengthened by the Mighty Jesus Christ of Nazareth.

AFFIRMATIONS AND ANTIDOTES

Britnie Thompson is the Director of Operations at Strap Em Up Boot Camp and a mentor to many youths in South Carolina. Since the age of 11, Britnie was a participant in youth ministry. At age 13, she earned a spot on the Conference Council for Youth Ministries. While serving in the ministry, Britnie gained leadership experience and discovered her passion to further lead youth in the upstate. She was hired as a secretary in the work study program at Greenville Technical College. While going to college, she made the Dean's List, became a Math Tutor, and from there, was hired as a part-time Bank Teller. She has experienced promotions and many positions in banking. Britnie has plenty of experience with financial literacy and administrative work. She is highly organized and professional.

Britnie's passion and calling is to help youth seek truth in who they are. They will learn to identify their inner-voice to have a voice in the community, schools, and their personal lives. Most importantly, they will learn how to grow spiritually.

I Can Be Content with Little

"Let your conversation be without covetousness; and be content with such things as ye have: for he hath said, I will never leave thee, nor forsake thee."
Hebrews 13:5, KJV

Affirming that I can be content with little tells me that it is God who gives me sustenance. He supports me. I am at ease of mind knowing that God will never leave me. He is my supplier. My needs are met. I am satisfied.

"Delight thyself also in the Lord: and He shall give thee the desires of thine heart."
Psalm 37:4, KJV

Affirming that I am satisfied tells me that I have confidence in the God who created me. I trust Him completely. I know the more time I spend in God's presence, I will experience great joy. I know God has great love for me.

I am Patient

"For I know the plans I have for you", says the Lord. "They are plans for good and not disaster, to give you a future and a hope."
Jeremiah 29:11 (NLT)

Affirming that I am patient tells me that I am willing to wait for the best. I know God has plans to prosper me and give me hope and a future. I know that I am created for a purpose. This gives me the strength to patiently wait on God.

I am Grounded

AFFIRMATIONS AND ANTIDOTES

Affirming that I have a solid foundation tells me that I am well-balanced. A well-balanced person understands education is needed. I heard the Word of God and apply what I hear to my life. I refuse to be confused about what God says about me and my purpose here on this earth.

I am Accomplished

Affirming that I am accomplished tells me I have goals and a plan to meet those goals. I make decisions that will help me be successful. I know to have success, I need to aim for a goal. My goals are obtainable because it is God who gives me strength to fulfill my purpose.

I am Stable

Affirming my stability tells me that I take ownership in my life. I will make good choices. I choose not to blame others and live in my past. I ask for forgiveness. I understand God's grace and mercy. I choose to make decisions that will advance me as a person.

I am Victorious

"I have told you these things, so that in me you may have peace. In this world, you will have trouble. But take heart! I have overcome the world."
John 16:33

Affirming that I am victorious tells me that I have already defeated my enemy. I will not give in to fear. My strength lies in my confidence that God has already overcome the world. Because of this, I am an overcomer. I am not defeated.

I am Rich

Affirming that I am rich tells me that my Heavenly Father is rich and I am His child. I will inherit that blessing. An inheritance is something that is passed down. It is transmission from parent to offspring. I am a child of God. I can never go broke.

I am Accomplished

Affirming that I am accomplished tells me that I am fulfilling my purpose on this earth. My purpose is to die to flesh and to be recreated by God. I am allowing God to recreate me into the woman He has designed for me to be. I have total confidence in God and His plan for my life.

I am Confident

"For I am confident of this very thing; that he who began a good work in you will perfect it until the day of Christ Jesus."
Philippians 1:6

Affirming that I am confident tells me that I trust God fully. I choose to have confidence in God, not in people. God will finish the work He started in me. I accepted Jesus Christ as my Savior. When God begins the work of salvation in me, He will finish it. God never starts anything He cannot finish. He said that I will be prosperous, and I believe Him.

I am Perfect

"I appeal to you therefore, brothers, by the mercies of God, to present your bodies as a living sacrifice, holy and acceptable to God, which is your spiritual worship. Do not be conformed to this world, but be transformed by the renewal of your mind, that by testing you may discern

AFFIRMATIONS AND ANTIDOTES

what is the will of God, what is good and acceptable and perfect."
Romans 12:1-2

Affirming that I am perfect tells me that I am a believer who is mature in Christ. Perfect does not mean I don't make mistakes; it means I am being transformed by God. I grow spiritually daily. My relationship with Christ gets stronger as I seek Him. Through Christ, I am made perfect.

My strength lies in my ability to make choices that will prosper my healthy, my charity, and my finances. I am to become spiritually, physically, and financially fit. There is a process to becoming fit. The beauty about becoming spiritually, financially, and physically fit is that all these things make you stronger. I've learned to be content with little. I've learned to be patient and enjoy my journey. I've learned to be confident.

Most of all, I've learned who I am, and I am happy with who I am. I have been made stronger, knowing that I am perfect. God created me for a purpose. He has work to get done through me. I want to be used by God. God takes the weak and makes them strong. My only job is to be born again. Daily, I tell myself that I am saved. I die to sin and God recreates me. I ask God to let my thoughts be His thoughts. I want my walk to be His walk. I am a reflection of God. God is Omnipotent and Omnipresent. My God is All-Powerful and everywhere.

I am a powerful woman of God. My source of strength comes from God's Word. Words speak life or death. I choose to speak life. These daily affirmations are my words that speak life to encourage myself and others.

Tieshsa C. Frontis is the founder and CEO of Know Your Self Worth, Inc. This organization, birthed in 2013, was created to inspire, uplift and teach women how God sees them and how they should see themselves through Him. She is a native of Charlotte, NC but relocated to Durham, NC in 1993 to pursue her college education at North Carolina Central University where she graduated with a dual BS in Chemistry and Biology. She believes education is important and is currently pursuing a dual MS at Pfeiffer College and will also pursue her Doctorate in Theology. She wholeheartedly believes in her movement, *Know Your Self-Worth*. She is a woman of purpose, faith and virtue, having persevered through diverse challenges including molestation, promiscuity, addiction, domestic abuse, miscarriage, homelessness, divorce and so much more. She lives to share her story with other women and men, encouraging them that they can make it and they can survive. She is a true testimony of resilience and triumph.

AFFIRMATIONS AND ANTIDOTES

Strengthen ME

I AM ME.

I AM becoming the person

I see because I believe in ME.

This reminds me that I first have to believe in who God is calling me to Be. I am my biggest cheerleader and encourager.

Psalm 139:14 - [14] I will praise You, for I am fearfully *and* wonderfully made; Marvelous are Your works, And *that* my soul knows very well.

Isaiah 40:31- but those who hope in the LORD will renew their strength. They will soar on wings like eagles; they will run and not grow weary, they will walk and not be faint.

Romans 8:37- Nevertheless, in all these things we are more than conquerors through him that loved us.

Draw strength in knowing that God created you to Be great. He made no mistakes when he created you. Loving and believing in you as you are will free your mind from negativity and believing the lies of the enemy or even the limitations you place on yourself. Continue to see yourself as being prosperous, beautiful, smart, and more than a conqueror. Because you must begin to **Believe** what you **See** in order for the **Manifestation** of **"You"** to **Be**.

Strengthen ME

I AM Great.

I AM destined for greater and all things I will obtain.

This reminds me nothing is off limits for me to have in my life.

Philippians 4:13- I can do all this through him who gives me strength.

Deuteronomy 8:18- Remember the LORD your God. He is the one who gives you power to be successful, in order to fulfill the covenant, he confirmed to your ancestors with an oath.

Take the limits off of your thinking. Your strength to endure and obtain favor is within the Lord and He has no limitations. You can be all that you desire and more. Your thoughts have power because they manifest into whatever you put into the atmosphere. You think Big and Greater, that's what you will obtain in your life but if you think small or of defeat than those are things you will have in your possession. "No"-thing is withheld from Gods sons and daughter in the Kingdom so, Go Get It!

AFFIRMATIONS AND ANTIDOTES

Strengthen ME

I AM a Powerhouse.

I am a producer that produces life through my words, my thoughts and my actions.

This reminds me, I have the power to create and shift the atmosphere or change my world with my words through my thoughts and actions.

Proverbs 18:21- The tongue has the power of life and death, and those who love it will eat its fruit.

Ephesians 3:16- I pray that out of his glorious riches he may strengthen you with power through his Spirit in your inner being.

Powerhouse according to Merriam Webster dictionary is:

1. a source of influence or inspiration
2. one having great power: such as

   one having great drive, energy, or ability

Your strength lies within you, your inner being and determination to be a great producer in your life. When you produce life, others can reap the benefits of your strength. You not only have the energy to live in abundance, but you will also find yourself being able to draw from that strength to overcome obstacles. Powerhouses don't give up they propel through the trials. Powerhouses don't wither away during rough times, but they rise above tribulation and find growth in defeat. Powerhouses don't dim their lights but shine bright in the midst of darkness. Powerhouses believe in themselves and are not shaken by someone else's success. Powerhouses understand the ability to stand tall in the crowd without making others feel inferior. You are a powerhouse full of strength, vitality and durability. Believe in yourself and go BE Great!

AFFIRMATIONS AND ANTIDOTES

BONUS:

7 Daily Strength Affirmations for You:

1. I am strong, and my self-worth is a source of my strength.
2. I will not let negative energy into my atmosphere. I control my world.
3. I may get weak at times, but God is my strength and refuge.
4. I am a source of influence and inspiration.
5. I see myself as greatness and nothing less is sufficient.
6. I know my worth and those that devalue it will be cut off at the root.
7. I am life and live life more abundantly.

VISIT SBG MEDIA @

www.thescatterbrainedgenius.com/publishing

Your words are your voice.

www.ingramcontent.com/pod-product-compliance
Lightning Source LLC
Chambersburg PA
CBHW050446010526
44118CB00013B/1709